DATE DUE			

The World Today

THE M. L. SEIDMAN MEMORIAL
TOWN HALL LECTURE SERIES

MEMPHIS STATE UNIVERSITY

*The M. L. Seidman Memorial Town Hall Lecture Series
was established by P. K. Seidman in memory of his late
brother, M. L. Seidman, founder of the firm Seidman and
Seidman, Certified Public Accountants.*

Publication of this ninth Series of Seidman Lectures was
made possible by a gift from Mr. P. K. Seidman to the
Memphis State University Press.

The M. L. Seidman Memorial Town Hall Lecture Series

The World Today

edited by Phineas J. Sparer

MEMPHIS STATE UNIVERSITY PRESS 1975

081
W89
96610
mar.1976

Library of Congress Cataloging in Publication Data

THE WORLD TODAY

(The M.L. Seidman memorial town hall lecture series; 1974-75)
CONTENTS: Salisbury, H. Toward a new world order.—Reasoner, H.
The news media—a service and a force.—Hayakawa, S. I. Education
revisited.
I. Sparer, Phineas J. II. Salisbury, Harrison Evans, 1908- Toward a new
world order. 1975. III. Reasoner, Harry, 1923- The news media—a service
and a force, the changing challenge to journalism. 1975. IV. Hayakawa,
Samuel Ichiye, 1906- Education revisited. 1975. V. Series.
AC5.W65   081   75-34486

ISBN 0-87870-028-5

The World Today

Preface

This is the first time since the inception of the M. L. Seidman Memorial Lecture Series that its Coordinating Committee decided not to select a new theme but to review and update three topics of utmost interest previously presented in the Series. The selections were by no means easy among so many excellent choices. In this year's search for a better understanding of our contemporary world, the Committee tried to engage the same speakers for the encore: Mr. Harrison Salisbury to review and bring up to date his discussion presented in 1968—*The U.S.S.R. in Today's World,* which he now captioned *Toward A New World Order;* Mr. Howard K. Smith, to review and update the subject he presented in 1969. However, as he was otherwise already obligated, the Committee was fortunate to engage Mr. Harry Reasoner, eminent news reporter and commentator, the topic still being *The News Media—A Service and a Force, The Changing Challenge to Journalism;* and Dr. S. I. Hayakawa completed the threesome, updating his original topic, *The University Under Attack* by the new title, *Education Revisited.*

Each of the three guest participants spoke from brief, prepared scripts that were modified and expanded during delivery at the time of the lecture and recorded on tape for subsequent transcription. For final publication, the editor consolidated each prepared script with the respective transcribed talk, doing it as meticulously as possible, for which the editor is solely responsible.

There were good reasons why this year's series was used to update some previously presented topics. To keep pace with rapidly changing events nowadays, information has to be continuously updated; and contemporary social and political developments are often quite baffling and frustrating. Questions arise. Did our guest speakers have access to adequate available knowledge; how well was that knowledge

interpreted or utilized for new insights or predictive purpose; and what about the flow of recent events and developments influencing new trends and future changes? Those
questions are dealt with explicitly or implicitly by the guest
speakers in excellent fashion; and they also amplify their
major ideas lucidly and succinctly. Nevertheless, there may
be value in some editorial comments.

Harrison Salisbury, outstanding newspaperman, assistant managing editor of the New York Times, and author
of books on Russia, China, and Hanoi among others, brings
his vast knowledge of world political affairs, often gained
firsthand, along with his keen thinking to focus on the
topic, *"Toward a New World Order."* He views and ana-
lyzes national and international situations, problems, and
policies with complete candor and objectivity. It is worthy
to note that it was Mr. Salisbury's candid and objective
reporting of the hard facts of the Vietnam War to the
New York Times that appealed to McNamara although the
articles were violently attacked by Defense Department
spokesmen and others in the Administration.

Looking back to his previous Seidman lecture, "Russia versus China: Global Conflict?" Mr. Salisbury had
already emphasized the enormous conflicting historical relationships between Russia and China. He now re-empha-
sizes their importance, bolsters and supplements his previous
analysis and poses some crucial questions relating to the
intensified rivalry of those two powers. He also ponders
possible world consequences if change should occur in the
dramatis personnae of either one or both of those countries,
especially because of the age factor in the top leadership.

Mr. Salisbury underscores "detente" as very significant
in our international affairs as he regards it to be our involvement with another powerful country in order to moderate mutual problems and promote better relationships.

Reference is particularly made to involvement between the United States and the Soviet Union, and between the United States and the Peoples Republic of China. He calls attention to the rather precarious but definite three-way balance interconnecting the United States, Russia, and China. And he points out the desperate necessity to forestall or stem the drift toward nuclear war. To facilitate this, American diplomatic efforts have been strongly concentrated and aimed at direct negotiations with the Soviet Union to halt the nuclear armaments race and even to abolish it. In that pursuit, Kennedy achieved the Partial Test Ban Trend, Johnson the Nonproliferation Treaty, Nixon the Salt I agreement and Ford the recent Vladivostock agreement. The latter agreement, according to Mr. Salisbury, places a ceiling on the total armory of nuclear weapons which either the Soviet Union or the U.S. might emplace and construct; and great progress has been achieved as it provides some warranty against the all-out course of a nuclear weapons race, and against the critical dangers that arise in this area where there are no safeguards whatsoever.

We thus come to view through Mr. Salisbury's insight and perspective the complexity of forces in world politics and diplomacy, and to wonder with him as to what course various nations will take under circumstances of imminent warfare, and how the United States would align itself if such crisis were to erupt between Russia and China, the latter due to become a genuine third super-power much before the end of this century.

Obviously, Mr. Salisbury suggests, the next imperative step should be for both the United States and Russia to welcome China within the framework of consultation, thereby creating a more united front in world affairs and in the attainment of peace. Mr. Salisbury also thinks that, in the not too distant future, Japan and other countries will gain super-power stature, although Japan has promised never to acquire nuclear arms. And he states that there are possibilities of a fifth super-power in the making with England and all of Europe, and perhaps a sixth will emerge in the Middle East. The world politics and ramifications of so many super-powers make the reading of Mr. Salisbury's full lecture most stimulating and timely.

Mr. Harry Reasoner—veteran newscaster, host of the "Reasoner Report," correspondent in Peking for its Emmy award-winning coverage of President Nixon's visit to China, Co-anchorman of Election Night Coverage in November '72 and the Presidential Inauguration in January '73, among his many journalistic functions—often speaks, like the other two lecturers in this series, from firsthand information.

He discusses and evaluates, in the present lecture, some journalistic experiences and the lessons learned therefrom for the best interests of the public and of the profession. In the very start of the talk, he directs his remarks at the Administration's campaign to discredit both the press and the objectivity of the commentators. Mr. Reasoner counters admirably Vice-President Agnew's attack on the news media and war critics in speeches at Des Moines and elsewhere. Agnew, unleashed and encouraged by President Nixon, charged that the networks and newspapers with multiple media holdings exercised such powerful influence over public opinion that they should vigorously endeavor to be impartial and fair in reporting and commenting on national affairs. Favorite targets, of course, were the Washington Post, Newsweek, and Mrs. Graham's TV stations. Threatening censorship of the news media, Agnew also rebuked the use of commentators with a preponderant "Eastern Establishment bias" and their failure to differentiate between news and comment. Mr. Reasoner indicates that he was duly upset about the credibility crisis that was emerging from the conflict between the Administration and the news media as a manifestation of the American way of life. And CBS, considering itself victimized by the scapegotism, viewed the public as apparently willing, like the kings of old, "to kill a messenger of ill tidings"—at the present time, CBS and other networks, liberal newspapers and press associations. Indeed, reporting bad news was unpatriotic. And support of the President was patriotic.

Reasoner's further comments on this part of the discussion are replete with revelatory glimpses, as are those dealing with Nixon's successful ruse to end the Vietnam War. Audiences were told that he had a special plan to end the war. But he implied he could not reveal it, as doing so might jeopardize secrecy. In point of fact, he had no plan at all. Because of subsequent conditions, well brought out by Mr. Reasoner, Mr. Nixon finally surfaced with a plan—*Vietnamization*. This called for the withdrawal of American troops in stages; there would be ever fewer Americans fighting on the ground, with ever fewer American casualties. Ever greater reliance, according to need, would be on American air power. Actually, Nixon was only putting a different guize on the war, for he still believed in its inherent mission; but to be honest with the American people was not his best policy. Interspersed throughout his lecture, Reasoner alludes to or reveals Nixon's penchant for the mere appearance of candor—even his shibboleth, Peace with Honor, when faced with Defeat. Clearly and plainly, it was the appearance of candor rather than candor itself that Nixon practiced and revered, and that ultimately led to his downfall, confounding and shaming himself. Mr. Reasoner is also concerned with raising journalism to a high level of professional attainment. That is why he is intensely sensitive to any outrageous practice in contemporary journalism. Hence his special delight in the demise of the expression "activist or advocate journalism," which refers to a fringe element in the profession that seeks to promote one's goals through a highly personalized use of the press. What made this personal equation a serious journalistic problem during the unrest of the '60's and Watergate is interesting to read in Mr. Reasoner's text.

He also points out significantly that we cannot, as human beings, completely divorce ourselves from the influences of our own education and experience. But he assures us that most serious practitioners of journalism learn early to be aware of and to minimize their effect. Indeed, to extricate oneself from the dire effects of one's education and experience, resulting in prejudices and prepossessions, is a challenge to a practitioner in any profession. It is generally known that education and experience determine what and how one observes or serves in life or fails to do so.

Dr. Hayakawa, past president of San Francisco State College, renowned semanticist and educator, is obviously quite enthused about the new campus scene and education revisited since he was last here in '69, when student activism still raged. Dr. Hayakawa's topic in that time of campus upheaval was "The University Under Attack." He now sees that the young people on campus have cooled it, have become conservative and have surfaced with refreshing attire and attitude that strongly contrast with those of the preceding years. Most striking is their increasing awareness that rioting and burning or blowing up campus buildings do not bring viable results but rather violently postpone orderly and peaceful change.

Dr. Hayakawa also views enthusiastically popular philosopher Eric Hoffer's penetrating criticism of contemporary education and his innovative proposals to make education more practical and meaningful to both the young and older people. The aim is to enlarge the role and direction of education for the good of the individual as well as of society. The young would pursue, of course, their *book learning* but they would also participate in the real life challenges that young people yearn for and need—applying their zestful energies in *experiential or empirical learning.*

Since education can never be isolated and considered apart from the life process, Dr. Hayakawa truly maintains "There's no doubt that books illuminate life. But if students are not permitted to experience life, what is there for the books to illuminate?" He thus wishes to liberate education from the confines of the classroom and to extend it successfully into the community, as a new dimension in education. For this reason, he applauds the recent rapidly growing movement of the experimental high schools and colleges throughout the United States that bring the students into the community and actively involve them in a variety of life situations outside the classroom: they are assigned chores in official city offices, jobs in factories, social agencies and so on, where they actually have tasks to perform. In that manner, the students qualify themselves by graduation time for both the high school diploma and the union card.

Dr. Hayakawa also commends the recent fantastic breakthrough in popular education with the proliferation of the community colleges as an integral part of our democratizing higher education. It began according to Dr. Hayakawa with the Morrill Act of 1862, which authorized land-grant colleges in every state of the Union. Today, more people than ever, especially from poor families are going to college—young and older men and women, including those married and having children. Older people are provided the opportunity to attend college. on a new basis, when they are more mature to benefit therefrom.

We are, apparently, in the midst of a veritable educa-

xvi

tion boom, with everyone reaching out for improvement through education, for a career or other worthwhile goals in order to enjoy life more humanely. That, indeed, is the very challenge of the ever greater democratization of education in a mass society—the art and science of cultivating humane living for all, instead of providing education for an elite.

Now, a few concluding remarks. In addition to having updated their respective presentations, our three lecturers have also upgraded their outlook. Each is staunchly optimistic of our country's future based on our historical heritage, our potential, and our experience in having come to grips with critical situations and challenges, both national and global. What comes through clearly and well in each of the lectures is that our national horizon has brightened because our shortcomings and strengths have been severely tested in recent years and appropriate solutions have been found.

Acknowledgments

The pleasure of rendering acknowledgments to people who have contributed vitally to the current lecture series is not without some trepidation. For omissions may occur inadvertently without displeasure intended.

Obviously, recognition is due Mr. P. K. Seidman, who wholeheartedly and elegantly memorializes his oldest brother by the formal Town Hall Lecture Series in perpetuity. And the editor cannot resist noting that P. K.'s warmheartedness is equally evident, as is his intellectual radiance, in his informal relationships.

Equal recognition is also due Memphis State University, for its distinguished sponsorship of this memorial and Dr. Billy M. Jones, President of Memphis State University, for his official as well as for his personal cooperation, and for introducing Dr. S. I. Hayakawa to this year's Town Hall audience.

Thanks are due two other persons for their respective contributions: Dr. John D. Jones, Vice-President of Student Affairs at Memphis State University, who introduced Mr. Harrison E. Salisbury; and Mr. D. A. Noel, Vice-President and General Manager of WHBQ Television, who introduced Mr. Harry Reasoner.

We are beholden, of course, to the members of the Coordinating Committee, who continue their endeavors quite assiduously in behalf of the Lecture Series; their names are appropriately listed elsewhere in this book.

Gratefulness is especially expressed to Dr. Festus Viser for expediting a variety of important but tedious tasks that are part and parcel of the success of the Lecture Series.

We are extremely thankful to Mrs. Reva Cook, who most ably publicized the Lecture Series.

The following persons also deserve our deep appreciation: Mr. Robert Garnett, for his untiring efforts in connection with the lecture hall arrangements; Mr. Robert S. Rutherford, for safeguarding the people and premises, in his capacity as Director of Security at Memphis State University; and Mrs. Barbara Lawhead, for her efficiency in transcribing the lecture tapes and in typing the manuscripts in preparation of their publication in this book.

Phineas J. Sparer
July 1975

Lecture One

by Harrison Salisbury

It gives me great pleasure, ladies and gentlemen, to be back in Memphis at the Seidman Lecture Series because it is a very distinguished one and I am delighted to have an opportunity to participate a second time and to try and bring up-to-date some of the observations which I made seven years ago.

It turns out that 1968 was a good watermark because it does provide a division between the two eras since World War II. I think 1968 is about the last year in which we lived in an international relationship which really derived from the great conflicts of 1939-1945. Since 1968 we have been constructing what for want of a better word I will call a new world order, but it is not the kind of order which we ordinarily have in mind when we think of a formalized system of world relationships; not the world order of the United Nations, but a world order based upon a super-power balance. What has really happened since '68 is that the two super-powers, the United States and the Soviet Union, whose relationship has, more or less, dominated the world since

1945, have embarked on a new and critical experiment to see if they can devise a framework, within which they can live, and resolve critical problems of the world by peaceful means without resort to a nuclear war, which without question, would destroy both of those countries and the rest of the world as well. There is no doubt that so far as the international sphere is concerned the Soviet Union and the United States have demonstrated to a considerable extent their ability not to go to war over third countries. One can only therefore rate the developments of recent years in a positive sense, despite qualifications, despite imperfections and despite the many dangers that overhang them.

One of these dangers, of course, is the possibility that 1975 will see a change in Soviet leadership. Mr. Brezhnev's health has not been too good and the rather precarious leadership structure of the Kremlin is now well into its eleventh year since the downfall of Krushchev. There are many signs that pressures are building up for a change at the top and changes at the top in dictatorial countries generally mean changes in policy as well. However, the Soviet attitude toward the United States is not based on some personal whim or characteristic of Brezhnev. It has enjoyed the wholehearted support of his colleagues. While changes may come with a shift in leadership, it is likely that they will make no more real difference in United States-Soviet relations than the change from Nixon to Ford did on the American side.

Along side the interplay of the two collossi, there has developed since 1970 a third protagonist in super-power relations — China. China is not yet the equal in strength of either Russia or America but compared to all other countries in the world she is clearly of super-power stature.

There has been great speculation and much discussion of the so-called "detente" between the United States and the People's Republic of China. But comparatively little thought has been given to the philosophical principles that underlie these problems.

I think this is the real significance of the dramatic series of events, many of which are deeply associated with the administration of former President Nixon. So, as Premier Chou En-Lai said to me when I was in Peking a couple of years ago, and the subject of Mr. Nixon arose, I said to him very frankly, that I was not a great admirer of the President, although I did support his foreign policy. The Premier said, and he has said it since then, that whatever else one might say about Mr. Nixon, one had to admire the basic tenets of his foreign policy. It was very natural for Chou En-Lai to say this because one of those tenets happened to coincide with his own (Chou En-Lai's) foreign policy, which placed us in a new relationship with the People's Republic of China.

What has happened actually is that the world today is in a rather precarious but quite definite three-way balance between the United States, The Soviet Union and The People's Republic of China. The story of how this has come about is really an interesting one and one which does mark a turning point in the world. I suppose the common denominator of all the events that we have seen, the dramatic trips to China, the summit conferences in Moscow and in this country — and there are more to come, as you know — since President Ford may be going both to Moscow and to Peking this year. I think the common denominator in this whole chain of events, really, was something which I spoke of when I was last here, namely the growing hostility between the two great communist giants, The Soviet Union and Communist China. This relationship between the two, which for many years had seemed to many people to be one of the strong points of the communist world, had begun to come apart about ten years earlier and while the most extreme degree of tension had not yet arrived when I was here in '68,

it was just around the corner in 1969 when the two countries came very, very close to coming, not only to blows with
each other, but into nuclear exchange along that 4500-mile
frontier that divides Russia and China. And it is out of such
hostility, which almost led to war on that occasion, which
has placed, as of today, more than a million Soviet troops
on the Chinese frontier and well over a million Chinese
troops on the Soviet frontier facing each other in one of the
world's greatest confrontations.

The hostility is so deep that China has emplaced all
or most all of her nuclear missiles in sites zeroed in on Soviet
targets in Siberia, and as far west as the Urals, and possibly
even further west; and the Soviet Union has emplaced what
are now permanent concrete silo installations of their missiles, zeroed in on Chinese targets. Out of that deep hostility,
and readiness for warfare on either side, has come an amaz-
ing alteration in top world-power relationships.

This hostility between the Communist giants coincided
with a period when American policy actively began to ex-
plore the potential of resolving as many as possible of our
major conflicts with each of these Communist nations and
setting up, in essence, a new kind of world super-power
structure. Essentially, what has occurred is that Washington
and Moscow have mutually agreed that the employment of
nuclear force in any super-power conflict is so mutually non-
productive as to be virtually unthinkable.

Hence, first steps were taken by the United States and
the Soviet Union. They were taken under the direction of
President Nixon, carried out through Secretary Kissinger;
and they had as their objective the general purpose of reducing the pace of the nuclear arms race and the overall
world expenditure for weaponry. They sought to institution-
alize, if possible, our relations sufficiently so that we would
not be moving through the latter part of this century always

tiptoeing past a possible new missile crisis, as the one which brought the two countries so close to nuclear exchanges back in the early '60s.

I don't know how successful this American initiative would have been, had it not been for the fact that the Soviet Union, filled with hostility toward China, with many of her leaders, and certainly a large portion of the Soviet high command, actively advocating a nuclear assault on China — if these men did not wish to assure that in any conflict which might arise with China that the United States would not be in China's camp.

Well, frankly, I don't think many Americans, and certainly not many official Americans, would have credited the idea that if war broke out between Russia and China that we were apt to turn up as China's allies. But this was a very real and potent fear on the part of the Russians, as I often had cause to discover in the course of prolonged discussions, not only with their top leadership, but their diplomats and many of my long-term friends and associates among the newspaper correspondents. They saw this as a genuine possibility. And so critical was the situation that they were willing to go a considerable distance toward accommodation with the United States to safeguard themselves, in the event that war should break out. And I think that this was the prime factor in making it possible to open up the path toward the resolution of the SALT I talks, toward the accomplishment of the whole series of nuclear agreements and treaties which, while far from perfect, do tend to limit the spread of nuclear arms and the usage of nuclear arms, as is provided through the treaty forbidding emplacing them on the ocean, on the beds of the ocean floors and other restrictions. Consideration of a non-proliferation treaty was a path which led straight to Vladivostock and the agreement announced after the discussions between Mr. Breshnev and President

Ford to place a ceiling on the total armory of nuclear weapons which either the Soviet Union or the United States might emplace and construct.

Now to be sure, there are many of us who are highly critical of the exact terms of some of those agreements. Some feel that the United States is giving up too much in one area; some are critical of our not demanding more from the Soviet Union; and many people are particularly critical of the last episode in this chain, the Vladivostock agreement, because of the obvious fact that the ceilings which are placed upon the United States and the Soviet Union are so high that it is going to take five, six, maybe seven years or more, of heavy construction, in both the United States and the Soviet Union, to build up to the levels which we've agreed now are the ceiling; and many people find it very difficult to understand why ceilings so high should be placed over a situation in which, for practical purposes, each side has something like parity at present.

But that is a difficult problem. The fact of the matter is that great progress has been achieved, and it does give us some kind of a warranty against the all-out course of a nuclear weapons race, and against the critical dangers that arise in this area where there are no safeguards whatsoever.

And simultaneous with our Soviet negotiations, there has been the whole series of dramatic moves, which has opened up our relationship with Communist China. It is probably difficult for some of you to recall that when I was last here there was no such thing as an American visiting Peking; there was no such thing as mainland Chinese in the United Nations; there was no such thing as exchanges or diplomatic contacts of any kind between these two great states of mainland China and ourselves. We were still in that frozen state which was the direct result of the Chinese intervention in the Korean War, and those years in which we and the Chinese were physically at war with each other. There was no change in the embargoes which we had imposed upon China; no change in the chain of alliances or in the bases that we had painstakingly constructed around China; and there was no change in our relationship with Nationalist China in Taiwan. I remind you of this because the circumstances today are so dramatically different. It is true that we have not yet established full diplomatic relations with Peking, but we are in Peking and the Communist Chinese are in Washington, and each has a liason office which, for practical purposes, serves all the normal functions of a diplomatic mission. We have, week by week, and month by month, and year by year, a growing exchange; visits of Americans now numbering thousands — I think the total American entourage which has visited China since the recent opening up of that country must be approaching ten thousand at the moment; and Chinese are coming over here, not in numbers of that magnitude, but substantial numbers of delegations, sports groups, entertainment groups, ballets, and others of that kind.

There is also a new atmosphere on both sides. No longer is China behind a wall. No longer is the United States the Number One Enemy of the Communist Chinese. Instead, we talk in civilized tones, in a sensible manner about our common problems. We have begun to trade. And perhaps what is most important, from the Chinese side, they now have a relationship with the United States which they firmly believe, insures the very reverse of what the Russians want. They believe in case of war between themselves and the Russians, that the United States is not going to wind up in the Russian camp.

I happen to think, and I think most of the people in this room would agree with me, that in the event of that war, we would never wind up in one camp or the other. There is no particular reason why we should. But the new fact, that we now have forged a chain of relationships with the Peking regime, acts as a block to the possibility of the outbreak of that great conflict, which the Communist states were so close to in 1969.

I might as well say at this point, that we have quite a ways to go with both of these countries before we can establish something which would be as secure as the kind of normal relationships which we have with the great Western European nations. But I don't think that is too surprising. After all, we are dealing with two great continental powers, each of which has, for many, many years been hostile to us, and towards which, we should remember, we have been hostile as well.

In the case of the Soviet Union, for many, many years, they openly had as their goal and their objective the overthrow of all capitalist states and the eventual spread of their particular doctrine to this country. Somehow, we didn't like that too well. And we don't move from a point like that to a point of a continuous interchange in fairly civilized tones, unless we have put in a lot of spade work, and unless there is a mutual reason for the development of a fabric of normal kinds of diplomatic interchanges. And that is, in essence, what we have done with the Soviet Union and what they have done with us.

Now let me give you a few examples of what it has produced. The world today is certainly not without threat of war. We know that. We know that it exists particularly in the Middle East. We know that because there'have been two wars in the Middle East in very recent times and, there are today, many who believe that there may be another war this spring. Now you might say this shows a lack of understanding between the United States and the Soviet Union because we are the two super-powers which have an interest in the Middle East, each of us with our satellite smaller powers of support in that area. The Russians with the Arab states, and ourselves with Israel. But there is another way of looking at it. I think it is a more important way of looking at it. That is, that in spite of the outbreaks of these two wars, despite the constant tension in that area, despite the very difficult nature of the disagreement, the Soviet Union and the United States have managed to remain in constant diplomatic touch over these issues for an extended period of years. They both have worked, perhaps harder in one moment, perhaps with some divergences in another, but each of them has worked in general toward the reduction of tensions in that area and, basically, against the outbreak of a conflict there which would produce a full-scale confrontation between the United States and the Soviet Union and thereby imply the possibility of nuclear war.

At this very moment, in spite of the obvious fact that Mr. Gromyko and Dr. Kissinger have differing ideas about how to go ahead with the next step in the Middle East, with Dr. Kissinger placing great store on his own shuttle diplomacy and his personal involvement with both opponents of the controversy; and with Mr. Gromyko rather preferring to see a new convocation of the powers in Geneva, yet each of them is working to prevent the outbreak of a new war in the Middle East.

They may not be successful, but my hunch is they will be; and that the overriding common purpose here, while it doesn't prevent the Russians from taking a poke at us when they think they can get away with it, we take a poke at them, too, when we think we can get away with it. Even though that does prevail, we do understand that the peace of the world is indeed our first preoccupation.

Now I point to another circumstance. For many years the United States was deeply and heavily engaged in Southeast Asia, militarily, with a state which was supported by both of the great Communist powers, competing against each other. But in spite of that circumstance, and the known fact that Hanoi was dependent on Peking for part of her arms and supplies, and upon Moscow for a great deal more, we were able to go forward, with both of those countries, and establish a better, closer and warmer relationship, while continuing to fight a state which was closely allied with the two of them.

That speaks for a great deal. There are many who say, "Well, why didn't the Russians, why didn't the Chinese, put pressure on Hanoi earlier so that the war could have been brought to an end?" Those people speak without very clear knowledge of the stubbornness and independence of Hanoi and its insistence on carrying on its own policy, regardless of their allies and their views of what Hanoi should do. I think that this circumstance, that we were able to move forward into a better relationship with the Russians, and the Chinese, at the very moment when this war was in its most agonizing phase, speaks a great deal more for the desire of both of those super-powers. Their primary desire was to get along with the United States rather than their willingness to pick up explosive material for use against the United States. For that reason I have an optimistic attitude toward the continuing efforts of Moscow and Washington to try and get along. I don't anticipate any massive breakthrough; I don't believe that Mr. Gromyko and Dr. Kissinger are going to work out a solution for the Middle East this spring, but I do believe they are going to make a certain amount of progress, especially when one considers how impacted that situation is, how impacted it was even before the rise of what really is now a different issue involving many of the same countries. And I'm talking now about the oil crisis and the oil-producing states of the Middle East.

Considering all those difficulties, progress has been made and more progress will be made, and we can watch this go forward. There can always be a misstep, a miscalculation, a sudden move by one side or the other, which can throw the super-powers off balance. But I think they have been through enough so that they will not be thrown off their balance so much that they would lead the world to its own destruction.

That is a positive attitude, so far as the Middle Eastern crisis is concerned, and I take very much the same attitude towards the oil crisis. It is a difficult one and a different one. This is not really a direct confrontation between the Soviet Union and the United States. It is a confrontation between the oil-producing states and the heavy consuming nations of the world — Western Europe, Japan and the United States. It is in a different atmosphere; and one reason why there has been no resort to force. There may be other reasons as well. But one overwhelming reason why there has been no resort to force in that area, and I do not expect that there will be (in spite of Dr. Kissinger's remark in December that "In case of strangulation, a nation would use arms to prevent itself from being strangled.")

The reason why I don't think it is going to move in that path is that it is perfectly apparent that behind the oil-producing nations, or most of them, stands the Soviet Union, in a sense as a sponsor and guarantor of those states, even though Russia herself has no particular direct involvement in the oil situation. I think that the remark that Dr. Kissinger made was an important one. I think it was designed to heat the situation up a little bit in line with his theory that you have to raise the temperature if you are going to get a solution. But from what I have been able to gather, in recent times, the general overall thinking in connection with oil is that it is perhaps not going to be as bad as we thought

it was going to be, or that somehow we are going to man-
age to learn to live with this situation, if not to like it, in
the next few years.

Though it is not entirely all bad that the Arab states,
among the most backward, for the most part, in the world,
get a heady infusion of capital, most of which will be spent
or invested in our country, it might begin to lift their civili-
zations up to something more closely approximating those
of the Western world. We shall see. It is a complex situation.
One that is difficult to predict. But the signs are not all
negative.

Now as far as China is concerned, we have indeed more
problems. We have not made the rapid progress toward a
resolution of all of our differences about China that were
expected when the Shanghai Communique was issued at
the close of Mr. Nixon's famous visit. The Shanghai Communique very clearly articulated our pledge to the Chinese
that once the tensions in Southeast Asia were reduced —
and this was a mere euphemism for our withdrawal of our
forces from that area — that we would move forward toward
reducing, if not eliminating, our rather substantial garrisons
on Taiwan, as a preliminary move toward the normalization
of diplomatic relations between China and Russia. For, despite the fact that we have missions in both countries, we
do not have normal diplomatic relations.

The reason we do not have normal diplomatic relations is a simple one. It results from the fact that we still
maintain diplomatic relations with Chiang Kai-shek. Mainland China has insisted, as a condition for establishment of
diplomatic relations, that each nation which enters into diplomatic relations with her, must break off diplomatic relations with Taiwan. Now it so happens that every one of the
great nations of the world have gone through this process,
and they are all now represented in Peking, except our-

r, there would be other par-
he Army in China today, as
to be in the power of strong
ild they back the new young
the older generation? Would
? Again, we do not know.
, and my Chinese friends con-
e Soviet Union is as aware as I
the Chinese situation, that this
take advantage of it, will change
hina — if not bring China back
at least create a sphere of Soviet

ed. No one can really tell at this
s are in the situation, too complex.
e situation might come to a head.
ise it is obviously to the advantage
at a regime in China, less friendly,
with the United States, come into
down the advantage which we now
deal directly, and individually, with
unist giants. I don't think anybody in
an bring the thing back together the
mpty-Dumpty fell off the wall; but if
half way back, they will have achieved
he world balance of power, it would be
ted States and a net gain for the Soviet

ge to us is really to try and nail down
Premier Chou En-lai, the forces which
relationship with the United States, the
stile to the Soviet Union, which are not
alliance. It is to our advantage then to
we can, obstacles to our closer relations,

selves. Many of them, have actually much closer relations
with Taiwan than we do. The Japanese, for example, with
enormous investments in Taiwan, with very, very close ties
— have followed through on this — and not to anyone's
great surprise. It has made very little difference to Taiwan,
or, to anyone else. The Japanese business in Taiwan has
continued to grow, and I foresee that it will go on growing.
It is soundly based, economically good business from both
sides, and the Chinese on the mainland do not interfere
with it, in fact, have made quite clear, informally, that they
like to see Taiwan prosper. Perhaps they think eventually
they will inherit this, but in any event, they say quite openly,
"We don't want to interfere. We did business in Taiwan.
What we're interested in is the diplomatic relationship."

Now the reason the United States has not gone forward,
outside of historical reasons that are deeply rooted back in
the MacArthur Era — a whole chain of circumstances that
I'm not going to go into at this time — really lie with our
special relationship with Taiwan, which stems out of our
treaty of defense. We are bound by our treaty of defense to
come to Taiwan's aid if she is attacked by the Mainland. We
have maintained this through the years, and of course, at
one period of time there was genuine feeling that there might
be such an attack. We have interpreted it to be in our interests to maintain a substantial air base in Taiwan. Very
important to us, really during the Vietnam War, but of no
very great importance to us at the present time. We also
have a substantial training machine in Taiwan, engaged in
training Chiang Kai-shek's troops — although I would suppose, after all these years, they probably might be training
themselves. After all, they have been on the Island since
1949. I should think they probably have a few people who
are capable of training troops, especially since they have
so many.

But in any event, like all of these things, there is a momentum of events that carries it along, and this is the establishment we have there, and naturally, the Nationalist Chinese do not want to break off relations. I don't say that I blame them a bit. They provide a problem for us. We have done nothing since Mr. Nixon was in China to move one step closer to creating the conditions that are necessary for full diplomatic relations.

Now this is the problem, actually, which faces Mr. Ford and Dr. Kissinger before the President's trip to China, which I understand is not going to be made until fall. Whether we will be able to figure out some manner of meeting the Communist Chinese demands, while not unduly offending the Chinese Nationalists, I don't know. One way, of course, of doing it would be to maintain the treaty, without having formal diplomatic relations. That sounds like a little sleight of hand, but it is possible. Actually the Chinese are quite good at sleight of hand. This might satisfy all parties, and subsequently enable us to move forward into the full diplomatic relationship.

Why do I emphasize "full diplomatic relationship" so much? I do it for the reason that there is in China a factor of instability in their regime and it stems from age of the leadership. We find that Chairman Mao Tse-tung is 81 years old, and while the Chinese often seem to think he is eternal, I have my own opinion about that, and I don't think he is, I think that he will disappear from the scene fairly soon. I mean within a year or two. It is just logical to expect that. His health is frail, although he certainly does see an occasional foreign visitor now and again.

Chou En-lai has been in a hospital in Peking since last spring. He is 77. When I last saw him, he was one of the spriest, most active, energetic men I've ever seen, and the things he has been doing while he has been in the hospital

In that struggle for powe
ticipants, notably the Army.
it has been in the past, tends
provincial commanders. Wo
radicals? Would they back
they fight among themselves
One thing we do know
stantly emphasize it, that th
am, or anyone who studies
age factor, and they hope to
the internal situation in C
into a viable alliance, and
influence in China.
This might not succ
point. Too many unkown
We don't know when th
But it is a danger, becau
of the Soviet Union, th
less willing to negotiate
power, in order to cut
have of being able to
these two great Comm
Russia believes they
way it was before Hu
they can even bring it
a great deal. And in
a net loss for the Un
Union.
So the advanta
the forces allied wit
believe in the close
forces which are h
looking for a new
eliminate, so far a

selves. Many of them, have actually much closer relations with Taiwan than we do. The Japanese, for example, with enormous investments in Taiwan, with very, very close ties — have followed through on this — and not to anyone's great surprise. It has made very little difference to Taiwan, or, to anyone else. The Japanese business in Taiwan has continued to grow, and I foresee that it will go on growing. It is soundly based, economically good business from both sides, and the Chinese on the mainland do not interfere with it, in fact, have made quite clear, informally, that they like to see Taiwan prosper. Perhaps they think eventually they will inherit this, but in any event, they say quite openly, "We don't want to interfere. We did business in Taiwan. What we're interested in is the diplomatic relationship."

Now the reason the United States has not gone forward, outside of historical reasons that are deeply rooted back in the MacArthur Era — a whole chain of circumstances that I'm not going to go into at this time — really lie with our special relationship with Taiwan, which stems out of our treaty of defense. We are bound by our treaty of defense to come to Taiwan's aid if she is attacked by the Mainland. We have maintained this through the years, and of course, at one period of time there was genuine feeling that there might be such an attack. We have interpreted it to be in our interests to maintain a substantial air base in Taiwan. Very important to us, really during the Vietnam War, but of no very great importance to us at the present time. We also have a substantial training machine in Taiwan, engaged in training Chiang Kai-shek's troops — although I would suppose, after all these years, they probably might be training themselves. After all, they have been on the Island since 1949. I should think they probably have a few people who are capable of training troops, especially since they have so many.

But in any event, like all of these things, there is a
momentum of events that carries it along, and this is the
establishment we have there, and naturally, the Nationalist
Chinese do not want to break off relations. I don't say that
I blame them a bit. They provide a problem for us. We have
done nothing since Mr. Nixon was in China to move one
step closer to creating the conditions that are necessary for
full diplomatic relations.

Now this is the problem, actually, which faces Mr. Ford
and Dr. Kissinger before the President's trip to China, which
I understand is not going to be made until fall. Whether we
will be able to figure out some manner of meeting the Communist Chinese demands, while not unduly offending the
Chinese Nationalists, I don't know. One way, of course, of
doing it would be to maintain the treaty, without having
formal diplomatic relations. That sounds like a little sleight
of hand, but it is possible. Actually the Chinese are quite
good at sleight of hand. This might satisfy all parties, and
subsequently enable us to move forward into the full diplomatic relationship.

Why do I emphasize "full diplomatic relationship" so
much? I do it for the reason that there is in China a factor
of instability in their regime and it stems from age of the
leadership. We find that Chairman Mao Tse-tung is 81 years
old, and while the Chinese often seem to think he is eternal,
I have my own opinion about that, and I don't think he is,
I think that he will disappear from the scene fairly soon. I
mean within a year or two. It is just logical to expect that.
His health is frail, although he certainly does see an occasional foreign visitor now and again.

Chou En-lai has been in a hospital in Peking since last
spring. He is 77. When I last saw him, he was one of the
spriest, most active, energetic men I've ever seen, and the
things he has been doing while he has been in the hospital

don't seem to me he has changed too much. It may well be that his illness is not so much physical as political. This has been a rather turbulent year in China. There have been many attacks on Chou and he has just come through the year with a stunning victory, ratified by the congress, the party congress which was just held in Peking, which brought Chou En-lai out on top.

Regardless of his physical state at the moment, his age also gives one pause to think. He is not, obviously, going to retain his vigor for too many more years. And when one looks around at the rest of that remarkable Politburo that they have in China, one is somewhat astonished to find that there are only three members who are under the age of seventy — one is in his sixties, one in his fifties, and one in his late forties, excuse me, in his late thirties (he's just a baby). You only have to have the chronology of these men to know that there is going to be a generational change in China fairly soon.

We don't know and I don't think the Chinese themselves know, who is going to come out on top. We hardly know the names of the men. It looks now as though Chou has solidified his leadership and that of the older generation for perhaps a couple more years. But the pressure from down below is bound to be mounting.

When the change does come, there will be, certainly, as there is in each Communist country, a struggle for power, in which different influences try to grasp the helm of that great state. While the most vigorous people are obviously these new, younger people in the Politburo, and the people whom they represent, basically the so-called Shanghai Mafia, that's what they call them — associated very much with Mao — a group of people who are extreme radicals and whose policies, were those radicals to come into office, we simply cannot predict.

In that struggle for power, there would be other participants, notably the Army. The Army in China today, as it has been in the past, tends to be in the power of strong provincial commanders. Would they back the new young radicals? Would they back the older generation? Would they fight among themselves? Again, we do not know.

One thing we do know, and my Chinese friends constantly emphasize it, that the Soviet Union is as aware as I am, or anyone who studies the Chinese situation, that this age factor, and they hope to take advantage of it, will change the internal situation in China — if not bring China back into a viable alliance, and at least create a sphere of Soviet influence in China.

This might not succeed. No one can really tell at this point. Too many unkowns are in the situation, too complex. We don't know when the situation might come to a head. But it is a danger, because it is obviously to the advantage of the Soviet Union, that a regime in China, less friendly, less willing to negotiate with the United States, come into power, in order to cut down the advantage which we now have of being able to deal directly, and individually, with these two great Communist giants. I don't think anybody in Russia believes they can bring the thing back together the way it was before Humpty-Dumpty fell off the wall; but if they can even bring it *half* way back, they will have achieved a great deal. And in the world balance of power, it would be a net loss for the United States and a net gain for the Soviet Union.

So the advantage to us is really to try and nail down the forces allied with Premier Chou En-lai, the forces which believe in the closer relationship with the United States, the forces which are hostile to the Soviet Union, which are not looking for a new alliance. It is to our advantage then to eliminate, so far as we can, obstacles to our closer relations, while there is in power in Peking a regime which has that same objective. In the long run, this could make a great deal of difference, not only to American foreign policy, but to the world balance of power. Because, as I said in the beginning, we now have a world — I wouldn't call it a world of three super-powers — China is not really a super-power in the sense that the Russians are, or ourselves. The Chinese don't have the clout, they don't have the industrial clout, they don't have the nuclear armory that either the Russians have or we have. But they are moving in that direction, and they are backed by something which neither the Russians nor ourselves have, which is the world's greatest population. A nation approaching one billion human beings, well-organized, good health, constantly being better educated, drilled in the discipline of the Communist Party, so that even though they don't have the physical accouterments of the Western World, they are able to accomplish great things simply with human labor, and they are moving ahead rapidly.

They will not be, in my opinion, a genuine third super-power much before the end of this century. When they *do* arrive at that point there is every indication that they will be not only the *third* super-power, but the *greatest* of the super-powers, simply because of their population total, the vast expanse of their territory, and their national pool of genius. Sometimes we forget that China is the oldest nation in the world, the oldest existing continuous civilization, with a history that goes back well over six thousand years. These people have been living together, working together, studying together, growing together, with a common language, a common culture, common ideals, and common objectives, and now, with a veneer of Communism, but a very important veneer. So far as skills and human talents are concerned, we have seen what happens to a medieval nation suddenly propelled into the modern world of technology in the case of

Japan. No nation has moved forward with the speed and rapidity of the Japanese, basically because of their organization, and the talents of their people. China provides a crew of talent, ten, twelve, fifteeen times as big as Japan, the largest pool of human resources in the world, and when that can be organized and moved in one direction, you have a power that is like nothing else in the world. That is the way the Chinese are moving — a long way ahead, if they don't fall apart. It is not likely that they will.

So the stakes are very, very, big in these very next few years. They may be very, very big in this particular year, because the pattern is being set, not just for the rest of this century, but for the next century in all probability. As Chou En-lai said, "No matter what else Mr. Nixon did, he pointed us in the right direction in our policy towards these two super-powers. It is now the question of carrying forward."

There are all kinds of problems in the world — the problems of economy or other problems at home, problems of our relationship with Europe, the problems of the relationships within Europe, the Middle Eastern problems, the problems of Japan, and the relationship between the Soviet Union and China, etcetra. I've described the latter in considerable detail — the tensions, the antagonisms, the hatreds, and the demands which each makes on the other. These are real. They work to our advantage because each of the super-powers has wanted to have a relationship with us. But they can work against our advantage and against the advantage of the world, in fact against the survival of the world should they become exasperated to the point that a nuclear war, which was averted in '69, should again come on the agenda of the relationship between the two countries. We sometimes think, I suppose, that conflict between two enemy powers, two Communist powers, is a good thing for us, but it is no good if it has the dynamite in it that might touch off a global conflict which would sweep over all of Asia and engulf the world.

And so lying ahead, beyond the regularization of our relations with China, the continuous momentum in our diplomatic interchange with the Soviet Union, lies this question of exerting our influence in some fashion to moderate relations between Russia and China. A very difficult thing to do. It goes back deep in their culture, deep in their history, long before either of them became communist; it involves exchanges of vast areas of territory, indeed, all kinds of factors. And we will have to apply our attention to such difficulties in the not distant future. No specialist however expects to see in our generation a renewal of the Sino-Soviet Alliance in active form. There are too many fundamental differences between the two countries to be resolved. Nor is it likely that the passing of Mao and Chou from power would cause a revival of fierce anti-American sentiment in Peking although it might cause some temporary aberrations.

The United States has dragged its heels so far as normalizing relations with Peking is concerned, largely because of an unwillingness to change its relationship with the Taiwan regime. However, some step in this direction may accompany Mr. Ford's first trip as president to Peking later this year.

In balance one must record the '70s thus far as a time of consolidation and foundation-laying in the new world of the super-powers. This by no means insures world peace but it does provide through continuous direct negotiation and interchange a manner of monitoring trouble spots and crisis situations that, with goodwill, can be with time institutionalized into a more reliable gauarantee of world peace. The next and most obvious step is some action by both super-powers to bring China within the framework of consultation and thereby seek to create a more united front in world affairs

and, hopefully, to modify the deep divisions that still divide
Peking and Moscow and which contain within themselves a
genuine threat to world peace should war ever break out on
the longest common frontier on the globe — the 4500-mile
line which divides the Peoples Republic from the U.S.S.R.

I said that this is the basic structure which is evolving
out of the last ten years. There are other things, which we
should look to, that will evolve before this century is over.
We have now two super-powers, one power which is perhaps
half as strong as those two, and then a whole bunch of powers considerably down the scale of values. But there are two
additional aggregates which will be pushing forward before
the year 2000. One of these is Japan — a country that shows
the most dramatic, economic and technological growth rate
which the world has ever seen. Some people think it is going
to be halted by the high cost of petroleum. I don't believe
it for a minute. I think that the pace of Japanese development is so great, the tempo is so great, that she's going to
move forward to new strengths, before too long, into this
super-power area. She is not as strong as the Soviet Union,
not as strong as ourselves, perhaps not as strong as China in
many ways, still without nuclear weaponry, still without an
armed establishment, but with a capability at any time of
developing nuclear arms if they want to, and probably developing nuclear arms the size of cigarette packages, such
being their talent for miniaturization. Eventually, the Japanese are going to join the Super-Power Club. At the moment they are psychologically alienated from it. They don't
want to be thought of as a super-power. They think their
destiny grows out of their nature, their skills and their technology, and that they are going to move into that circle
sooner or later.

The other aggregate pushing forward before the year
2000, but in a sense perhaps even more of a question mark,

is Western Europe which has all the capability, all the potential, if the countries within it come together, of equaling
any one of the states that I have mentioned, and even perhaps, being superior to it. We think of Europe as being a
divided place, an area where Italy seems on the verge of
bankruptcy. We can't figure out what the future of England
is going to be. Germany always seems to win the tricks, and
the French are very selfish and very rich. All those things
are true, but all of Europe is now bound into economic associations, which have been deeply profitable to Europe.
Their political ties grow stronger and stronger. Through the
framework of NATO they have a political organization and
a military organization. What is lacking now are two or three
more steps forward until the momentum of the creation of
a unified Western Europe in political structure of some variety begins to emerge. It may take ten or twenty years, but
I feel certain that we will see it in this century. And when
it happens, there will be a fifth super-power which may be
the greatest, the most skilled, the most able, of them all. I
think the chances are that there are going to be five great
states in the world, and perhaps there will be a sixth. Perhaps
with all the money they are gathering in, there will rise in
the Middle East another complex. I can't see that yet, but,
who knows what the future may bring.

All this means that while we have a new structure, new
balances, new responsibilities, new safeguards, we also have
new challenges and new dangers, because if the politics of
two super-powers are complicated, and we know this since
we play that game with the Russians; and the politics of
three, with the Chinese included, are even more complex,
and we can see some of that because we have rudimentary
games going on. The politics of four super-powers and five
super-powers add a great deal more complexity. This means,
from our standpoint, that any dream we may have of turn-

ing back to ourselves, to an idyllic dream of an America
which never really was, to concerning ourselves only with
things within our own country, perhaps of having a fortress-
America, or something of that kind, are idle. The rules of
the game have been set and we are one of the players; one
of the great players, and how well we play that game has a
lot to do with how strong we are and what kind of a quality
of life we are going to have in our own country. If we miss
a bet, or we miss the stakes in the game of two, or the game
of three, it will be that much harder to catch up in the game
of four, and most difficult in the game of five. We have
more advantages than any other player in the game. At the
present time we have a one-to-one relationship with the
Soviet Union; a one-to-one relationship with China. Western Europe is our friend. Japan is our closest ally in many
respects. We have a chance, through the rest of this century,
of maintaining that dominate position in the world. We may
not want to dominate the world. I hope we do not wish to,
but the dominate position is valuable, so far as protecting
what is dear to us here in the United States is concerned.
But it is going to take great skill. It already takes great skill.
Whatever we may think of Dr. Kissinger, however we may
criticize him, or make jokes about him, he has shown enormous skill in playing this particular game. How many other
players do we have? How many are we developing? How
well are we, the great American Public, aware of the complexity of the stakes in this game to enable us to give the
support which our government needs in critical moments?
How aware are we, when the government makes a mistake,
how quickly can we pick it up? How quickly can we exert
our influence to prevent the enormous waste of our resources
in the gambit which is certain to lose? These are the kind
of questions which we as Americans must be asking ourselves, now. Along with all the other questions which are on

our minds — economic questions, political questions, questions about the fabric of our country. You may say they are too great. The burden is more than we can take. I don't believe that for a minute. I think we have the resources here. I think we have more talent and capability than any other people in the world. We are further advanced technologically, educationally, in almost anything else. We have the cards in our hands. If we cannot, with those resources, keep ourselves ahead, and play the game intelligently, who can? I think we can do it. I think it is something which all of us, not just one person, not just a small group in Washington, not merely the man in the State Department, or the White House, or the Pentagon, or Congress, or all the people in Washington — it is too big for them. It is personal for all of us. We are going to have to join in it. It is time to start right now.

"The News Media — A Service and A Force,
The Changing Challenge to Journalism"

Lecture Two

I like the idea of this lecture series, and I am proud to
be a part of it. I prepared myself by looking over the record
of an earlier series, and in the preface to the publication of
the 1969 Seidman Lectures which were called, *The News
Media — A Service and A Force,* Dr. Viser noted that the
topic grew out of the unpleasantness at the Democratic National Convention in Chicago, a year before that, in 1968,
which, as we all remember, was not a vintage year. Dr.
Viser noted that the one effect of the tumult was that significant numbers of the general public, for the first time
began to question the objectivity of the news media, particularly the condemnatory pictures that have been seen on
television at various times.

And I'd like to talk about that briefly because I think
it is pertinent to what has transpired since then in our profession, or craft, or racket, or whatever you choose to think
of it as, but which has become so important to all of us.
My friend, and former colleague, Mike Wallace put it this
way. He said, "The public simply did not want to believe

the evidence of its home screens. I was there, one of the hundreds of reporters in the violent streets of Chicago. Individually our eyes saw only small parts of the story, but collectively, I believe, we saw all, or most of it." I too was there and I agree with Mike. Nevertheless, the outrage of the public response was withering and surprising. Television news bore the brunt of it, but no part of the press escaped the anger. I was working at CBS at the time, and the letters about television reporting on the Chicago Democratic Convention came in by the many, many thousands, and they were eleven-to-one condemnatory of CBS.

The media did not go unnoticed, like some politicians, including those concerned with the election of Richard Nixon. Within ten months after his inauguration in 1969, just a few months after the 1969 Seidman Lectures, the administration began its calculated campaign to discredit the press and to exploit, we believe for its own ends, the public doubts about our qualifications and our objectivity. That campaign, you may remember, began with Spiro Agnew's speech in Des Moines, a speech which was written at The White House, complaining about instant analysis and querulous commentators. It irritated me particularly in a personal way, at the time. I remember because I am from Iowa and I resented this man from Maryland going out to my state, believing that that is where the hicks were who would swallow anything he wanted to give them.

He spoke then, and at other times, about an "effete corps of impudent snobs", and he followed it up with beauties of alliteration like "gnattering nabobs of negativism", and the like. I wonder what ever happened to Spiro Agnew?

Anyhow, while Agnew took care of the words, other administration officials were handling the sticks and the stones. Charles Colson. was opening up another front, privately, in the corporate executive suites that are connected with the media, with arrogant threats of the financial consequences that the television networks would suffer if their news departments did not ease up on Watergate. But the real muzzle, and the thing that seems quite terrifying to a lot of people in journalism and broadcasting, was being used by a man who wasn't all that well known, an aide of Mr. Nixon's called Clay Whitehead. He was handling the attack on I guess what you could call "the soft underbelly of broadcasting", if Mr. Noel doesn't object. It is regulation by the government through the Federal Communications Commission. Whitehead left no room for misunderstanding of what he was doing. He said, "Stations and networks would be held fully accountable at license renewal time." Before he finally left his job, he also devised a plan to create sixty-seven major television stations and formed them into a new network.

The FCC's power to revoke licenses understandably worries a lot of broadcasters. When someone else has the power to shut off your livelihood you tend to listen to him. I don't think that broadcast journalism, which is only a part but a major part of all broadcasting, will ever be fully free and able to develop until it is taken out from under any kind of FCC control and given exactly the same status under the First Amendment that the newspapers have. Dr. Frank Stanton, the former president of CBS, called the administration's campaign "The gravest threat to freedom of the press since the Alien and Sedition Laws of 1798," which was a long time ago.

We wonder why this campaign came about. I suspect one reason is the nature of Richard Nixon himself, that puzzling man. The entire record of his public life showed him, whether you approved of him or disapproved of him,

to be uncomfortable with the press, always wary and sus-
picious of reporters, maybe with some reason.

I think there are other more specific reasons why the
campaign against the press began. When Agnew spoke in
Des Moines, the press was beginning to ask questions about
the secret Nixon Administration plan to end the Vietnam
War, the promise of which was probably more responsible
for the narrow presidential victory that Mr. Nixon had in
1968 than any other single factor. "What is this plan?"
people were asking. "What is it and when and how will it
end the war?" It appears clearly now there never was a
plan, only the confidence of utmost ego that he could bring
it about. A discredited press, intimidated, and on the de-
fensive, might ease off on those important questions about
the plan and its nature; and might not look too closely at
the other things that we now know were going on. And if
it didn't ease off, if it were discredited, its reporting might
not be believed.

When Merriman Smith spoke to you in May 1969, that
superb reporter put his finger on what I believe to be
another reason for the government campaign against the
press. He observed that some responsible Washington officials thought some of the money paying for the dissent
and violence, and there was a lot of it, on the campuses
and across the nation, was coming from Mainland China;
and he added, responsible men and women in Washington
also feared that, in the summer of 1969, the various elements of dissent, which had been dangerous enough, and
violent enough but disorganized, might merge.

The White House testimony in various cases, and the
White House tapes, have made clear that the Administration's concern for that dissent amounted to an obsession, if
not a paranoia. I would like to say to some of the younger
people in the audience, or some of those with poor mem-

ories, it is not as completely un-understandable as you might think, there were some scary things going on in the United States in 1967, '68 and '69. But the Administration felt that to an extreme degree, and in that feeling were the seeds of the pattern of immoral, and illegal, and improper activity that has come to be known, in general, as Watergate. Here were the seeds of subversion of various government institutions — the CIA, the FBI, even the IRS — for political purposes they were never meant to serve, although it was certainly not clear at the time. In this obsession and paranoia were also the seeds of Richard Nixon's own downfall.

That is how things stood with the nation and the press as we emerged from the Sixties, which included the longest period of national soul-searching and internal-questioning that we have ever gone through. It seems to me that as we entered the Seventies this country was in a way like an individual ending an extremely long binge. We had been for this length of time engaging in a kind of behavior not characteristic of American history, something new, with the exhilaration during that time of something like a drunk, doing things he had never done before. So now we were like a man waking up in the morning and saying, "My God, what have I done?" Like a hangover. And like a hangover sufferer, we tended to move very carefully and slowly in seeking some basic reassurance that we could live, get through somehow, that we could do our job. Historically, eras and that kind of national change don't take place in a moment. Turning points take years. I think 1968 was the start of the turning point. In the mid of all the turmoil came the election of Richard Nixon. He didn't bring an awful lot of people to the polls. There was a low turnout, and he won with something like 23% of the eligible vote, not exactly a mandate. But it was, nevertheless, almost as if there were a tangible sense of relief in this country that we had been able to elect a president at all, that somehow the Republic was going to survive.

I remember after the election in 1968, remembering an old *New Yorker* cartoon as I thought about the country, a cartoon that showed a very, strange-looking man standing outside a hospital delivery room and the nurse had just come out and said to him, "Congratulations. It is a baby." If I thought of it at that time, I didn't even think of it in terms of any reflection on Richard Nixon, but just the startling surprise that we had been able to do it, after all we went through in 1968.

Following that, we did get through a relatively quiet four years. Dissent did begin to die down, or at least to express itself in more constructive ways. And then in 1972, Mr. Nixon got his landslide, the largest popular vote margin in history. Some strange activity went into the getting of it, however, but we didn't know about it then, and I don't think that that really is relevant. Without even any of the strange activity, he would have won by a landslide. And with that landslide, the cult of the all-powerful presidency reached its zenith. A cult and a concept that probably was planted, at least in my professional lifetime, with Franklin Roosevelt. It certainly bloomed profusely with Lyndon Johnson, and bore its bitter fruit with Richard Nixon: Watergate.

What happened with that landslide was that the non-elected types, the key people who never ran for office, but who had so much influence in the Nixon White House, thought they had gotten the mandate to fix up everything, to tidy up all the ridiculous loose ends that the American process had left in two hundred years. It is interesting to remember the cast of characters who got involved in Watergate, and there are two significant, at least there are two startling elements: one is that they were almost all lawyers; and, secondly, that with the single exception of Richard Nixon himself, none of them had ever been elected to anything. I suppose what that means is that people who get elected to office, if they are not more honest than other men, at least develop a sixth sense of what they can get away with.

Lyndon Johnson, when he took over from John Kennedy after the assassination, was talking one night to his old friend, Sam Rayburn, Speaker of the House, and he was bragging about the intellectual quality of the Kennedy staffers who had agreed to stay on in the Johnson White House, saying what a fine and fascinating group they were; and Mr. Rayburn is supposed to have said, "There is just one thing, Lyndon, I wish one damn one of them had ever been elected dogcatcher." One particular arrogant group of non-elected officials in the middle Sixties got us into Vietnam, and the other arrogant group of non-elected officials from 1968 on, forced their leader and boss into a situation where he had to become the first president in history to resign.

However in 1972, after the landslide, we didn't really know about Watergate and we didn't know all the profound ramifications of the scandal that would be revealed to a generally incredulous America. The system worked, the courts and the Congress, and to some extent, the press, did lay the scandal bare. But another part of the system, the free press, had to coax a reluctant and foot-dragging America into acceptance of the overwhelming weight of the evidence. And even now that they have the "smoking pistol" in the White House tapes, some people still don't want to believe.

Watergate demonstrates what seems to me one of the cardinal rules about the exercise of power, whether it be political or other. That is, power is limited only by the restraint of the person who wields it, which you cannot count on, or it is limited by the challenge to the wielding of it, which in our system you *have* to count on. But the Democratic Congresses' almost servile acquiescence to the Republican president for some four years and the pattern of conduct of the Nixon White House, demonstrate that there certainly had been very little challenge and damn little restraint, and the challenge that is presumedly built into the system didn't operate for awhile.

Until Watergate broke open, power was running amuck. One of the worst things about it was that Watergate sharply set back a process of healing in this country which I think had begun under President Nixon. I don't speak as a protagonist or antagonist, but the country had begun to heal, had begun to move together. And then Watergate really set it back.

I think what had happened in 1972, in that mandate, as I read it, was America saying: "Look, the middle is speaking. The middle is taking over." America was saying to the New Left: "No, thanks. Wait. Meld yourself into the political process of this country as dozens of even more radical movements have done before you, but don't try to bomb your way in. We won't buy that." And too, what was left of the Far Right, the country was saying: "No, we don't want your way either. We don't want to retrogress to something that we rejected back in the 1930s." I think we were saying in an inchoate way, "Let's get back to the middle that has always been the strength and the direction of this country, and let's get the country back together again." That is what we wanted. But what we got was Watergate.

Stated bluntly, with Watergate, Richard Nixon so grossly offended our middle-class morality that he could never again merit our trust. We are, I think everyone in this room, and most of the people that we deal with through the day, we are of the bourgeoisie. We are the middle class. We are in America the largest middle class in the history of the world. No other country and no other social system has ever produced so many bourgeoisie as ours, and it is a word, as you know, to a lot of people, pejorative. But our system made it and we've got to live with it. Our system made the class, produced the Babbitts and the Snopes, and the E. Howard Hunts. But it also produced the Lindberghs, the A. Phillip Randolphs, and the Neil Armstrongs, and the Jonas Salks.

Merriman Smith, when he talked to you six years ago, remarked on the impending reaction of the middle class, sensing how imminent it was. He said then: "If our country is swept by unrest, violence, and the challenge of authority, it is not an entirely hopeless situation. There is, in this frequently distasteful process, an element of growth, possibly a moral improvement." I think they were prophetic words. He was speaking of activity outside of government and could not know of equally distasteful abuses even then beginning within government itself. But how prophetic! Dr. Daniel Boorstin, the eminent historian at the Smithsonian Institution, believes that the purgative effect of Watergate has been much what Merriman Smith sensed. In Dr. Boorstin's words: "It has dramatized the power of Congress. It has dramatized the integrity of our Courts and it will probably have the effect of making anybody who sits in the presidential chair be more scrupulous of his use of the government — of the powers of the presidency."

My colleague, Howard K. Smith, in his Seidman lecture, spoke of the problem of governmental procedures that were invented for a rural nation of eight million people now being applied to a highly urban nation of over two hundred million people. And Howard said: "I think we

need some changes so that Congress will be more sensitive
to what the people need and what they want."

I would like to think that Watergate began that
process of change. It has jolted Capitol Hill out of its cus-
tomary complacency. The senators and representatives, even
if it is purely for their own survival, show signs of paying
more attention to the voice of the people. The venerable
seniority system has been challenged successfully in the
House; some closed doors have been opened. Election and
campaign procedures have been somewhat reformed, particularly in the vital area of financing presidential cam-
paigns. And Congress is now taking tentative steps toward
a more streamlined and responsible system for dealing with
government spending.

I realize nobody ever got a bad reputation as a prophet
by being pessimistic about what the United States Congress
would do, but there are some signs that they may do something in the next few years. Why, just this week, I think,
the Senate began its Easter Recess, but they haven't had
any time off at all since Christmas, except for Valentine's
Day Weekend and a couple of other things. They are engaging movement in the right direction and I hope they
will realize how much more has to be done.

The times cry out for more; demand it. This inter-
woven problem of the economy and energy that we have
become so conscious of in the last eighteen months, that
so dominates the news and will for years to come — re-
quires a government sharply attuned to the needs of the
people and far more quickly responsive to those needs.

It has been a substantial danger in this country for
several years that we might slide into another Great De-
pression, or one that would make the previous one look
pretty good. We cannot allow that to happen. We cannot
allow Americans to suffer from hunger that can be fed,

from pain that can be eased, from idleness that could be put to work. The news media, both as a service and a force, have a responsibility here. I am sure we will meet that responsibility, whatever shortcomings we may have. Neil Sheehan of *The New York Times* is probably best known to most people as the reporter who obtained The Ellsberg Papers in the Vietnam War, those papers which had such a catalytic effect on the Nixon White House. Neil was also a very fine Vietnam War correspondent and he wrote a book, *The Arnheiter Affair,* about Lt. Cmdr. Marcus Aurelius Arnheiter and his attempt to clear his name after having been abruptly and summarily removed as Captain of the USS Vance after three months of command in Vietnam. In the book, Neil spotted one of the internal problems of the press. He called it a kind of hardening of the arteries: "a tired community of hemmed-in reporters, editors who ask the wrong questions, publishers who are more interested in profits than in the quality and accuracy of the information that they print." He wrote of the way the public relations man and the government propagandist had learned to exploit this hardening of the arteries by keeping an eye on the deadline: a few scribbled notes, quickly turned into some readable form and rushed into print against the ticking of the clock, all with too little thought, and too little time for thought.

Neil Sheehan called this an anachronism that results in the daily publication of falsehood and bias in favor of those who best know how to exploit this weakness in the press. It is such an anachronism. Though he was writing of newspapers, I can give you a classic example of how the same exploitive technique was used against television news. It occurred on the day the Supreme Court, unanimously and in an opinion written by Mr. Nixon's own Chief Justice, struck down the former president's claim of executive privilege and ordered him to surrender the subpoenaed White House tapes.

Mr. Nixon was in San Clemente when that ruling came down
in the morning and the big question was would the president
defy the Supreme Court? Through the day the White House
kept promising to make an announcement, but none came.
Finally reporters at San Clemente were summoned to meet
with Mr. Nixon's chief defense lawyer, James St. Clair. The
session was scheduled to start at a time coinciding exactly
with the beginning of the TV network evening news broad-
casts. The ploy was obvious. It was to put the cart before
the horse. For Mr. Nixon, who was at that time still engaged
in what he hoped would be a successful fight, the Court's
decision couldn't have been more devastating. Indeed, it
started his final slide from office. Scheduling Mr. St. Clair's
announcement at that time was an attempt to put the best
possible face on a terrible situation. Since most of the nation,
for good or evil, gets its news from television, you thus project to the nation the image that this is a president who obeys
the law, ahead of the image of one of the three co-equal
branches of government ordering him to obey it.

It was a technique which, in variation, the Nixon Administration used many times in its long fight to survive
Watergate and a technique, which in all fairness it should be
said that other presidents have used, Mr. Johnson was particularly fond of making big announcements at 7:02 P.M.,
New York time.

Perhaps the other side of the hardening arteries coin
that Neil Sheehan was complaining about might be the ex-
cessive journalistic zeal that Watergate spawned. With the
example of Bernstein and Woodward of *The Washington
Post* before them, there was a rush of reporters to investigate
anything and everything. This is not to say that a lot of things
they were investigating didn't need investigating and more
will need investigating. But for a time I think we saw a
dangerous shift in emphasis from the story itself and the

value and importance of the story to the method by which the story was obtained. It was a real front page, hot damn! Look what we dug up!

That seems to be passing now, and the passage is probably the result of the intense and continuing self-examination that Watergate forced journalism to make of itself; an examination of not only past practices, but also of the way we handled the Watergate story itself. I could never convince you of the amount of time spent in solitary reflection by those of us who dealt with the news of Watergate in the last couple of years. It was obviously an unfolding story of intimidating magnitude, completely out of anything else we ever had in our experience, almost beyond our imagination. So the continual question had to be: Are we being fair? And to fuel our own second thoughts, the White House kept telling us, "No, you're not being fair," even as the tragedy was removing from office the Vice President of the United States and the President of the United States for criminal activity, and had indicted the former Attorney-General of the United States and was sending to prison a host of other once powerful men.

The press' Watergate self-examination, I think, also contributed to the demise of another expression of journalism that I am glad to see die, "activist journalism." There has always been, and I guess always will be, a fringe element in our profession that seeks to promote its own goals through a highly personalized, highly subjective use of the press. The unrest of the '60s so increased the size of, and so focused attention on, this element that some responsible publications were tempted to take it seriously. Not any longer. No intelligent editor wants a reporter who becomes a part of his own story, a participant in and advocate of the cause that leads to the result. Just as Watergate has started to wipe out the establishment lackey approach to the news, so has it been hard on activist, or advocate, journalism, and none too soon. I don't mean to ask you to think that the press has completely purified itself of its sins of omission or commission. I do think we have been made more aware of, and more on guard against, our sins just as the country has.

In my reference a moment ago to the highly subjective nature of activist, or advocate, journalism, I meant no disparagement to some other remarks made to an audience here by Osborne Elliott in his Seidman lecture. He said, he talked about the problems that he ran into in being in one particular campus story in three roles — a trustee of a university, a visiting professional newsman and the father of a student son there — and he said that he chose to solve that unique dilemma by dropping the roles of being trustee and reporter, and just being a father — standing aside as a newsman.

I know, and you know, that we cannot, as human beings, completely divorce ourselves from the influences of our own education and experience. I do think, however, that most serious practitioners in the profession of journalism learn early to sort of identify and watch for their own personal influences; to minimize their effect, to leave their prejudices on the airplane, or at home in the morning. Most of us in the news business never find ourselves in a situation to require an action as drastic as Osborne Elliott had to take, but we do frequently have to act consciously to balance unconscious influences and to seek, as does a juror, to put personal prejudice aside and to reach our particular daily verdict on consideration of only the evidence before us.

I found it especially appropriate to discuss this subject with you on what is rapidly becoming the eve of our nation's two-hundredth birthday. It was, after all, our Founding Fathers who wrote into the Constitution the guarantee of free speech and a free press, and thus gave to the news media a role and a responsibility as a service and a force. As a na-

tion we certainly have problems as we face our second two
hundred years, including whether we are going to be able
to finish our first two hundred. But as we look back over
the first two hundred, we see that somehow, the United
States has always faced up to its problems. Sometimes the
answers didn't come as fast as they should have, but sooner
or later, somehow, the answers did come.

As we move on, we are going to be looking for a lot of
new answers for the time that is left to each one of us, and
our kids are going to be looking for a lot of even newer answers to newer problems in the first decades of our next bi-
centennium. I will be, you will be, and they will be, looking
for those answers and that is what our country is all about.
I think very often, with considerable emotion, about the
United States which has been good to me, and I think good
to humanity, in the time I have seen it in the Twentieth
Century. And I think about what other people around the
world have thought about us, and I remember noticing a
few years ago, in *The New York Times* on the occasion of
the fortieth anniversary of Charles Lindbergh's flight to
Paris, when they had some kind of a celebration in Paris.
The *Times* had a story on it and they reproduced on their
front page, the front page that they had run that morning
in May of 1927, after his flight and one little item on the
front page intrigued me so I got a magnifying glass to look
at it and it was a sidebar on something that had happened
late at night, after Lindy had landed, and there had been
the celebration and he had gone to bed. Everything was
quiet, except that a mob formed in the street in front of the
American Embassy and they demonstrated until the Ambas-
sador came out on a balcony and granted their demands. He
brought out an American flag because they wanted to
cheer it.

In the years between 1927 and 1975 we have gone

through some periods of time when there wasn't much cheering for the American flag around the world. But I would like to think that by the time of our two-hundredth birthday and the years to follow that we will all behave so well they will cheer it again in various places.

Lecture Three

by Dr. S. I. Hayakawa

One of the things I like about Memphis, of course, is its strict moral standards, as exemplified in a famous saying in a blues song, " . . . Mr. Crump don't 'low no Easy Riders here." And, of course, there's a more carefree side to the Memphis character which is exemplified in a further line in the same song, " . . . we don't care what Mr. Crump don't 'low, we gonna barrelhouse anyhow." And both sides of your multi-faceted character, I appreciate.

Dr. Jones and I were comparing notes, before we came in, on our experiences as president; and it seems he became president of Southwest Texas Teachers College in September 1969, and by October he was in Federal Court, having to defend his actions. I said, "Why was that?" He said, "Well, I tried to imitate what you did in San Francisco State." I said, "It serves you right, you fascist pig!" So, we're fraternity brothers, after a fashion.

Wherever I go I'm asked these days how things are going now on college campuses; and things are very, very quiet, I explain. That's why I'm out of a job. But I can best answer the question by quoting from a letter I received recently from a professor of Drama at Hamilton College in Clinton, New York. He says, "The young at Hamilton continue to amaze me. Last week my wife and I received an engraved invitation to a "Tea", at one of the fraternities, and it said, "semi-formal". We didn't believe it but we went and there were four young hosts in morning coats and striped pants with carnations in their lapels. The tea was Earl Grey, and there were two girls in long dresses and lovely 1930's hats pouring. The faculty guests looked extremely nervous for a while, but it ended up as the nicest, non-alcoholic bash I've ever been to in years. A visiting college president from elsewhere was in attendance and when I asked him his impressions he replied that he enjoyed the tea very much, but, he said, "What the hell's happened to the younger generation?"

It was in September 1972 that I heard the following conversation in our Administration Building at San Francisco State University. Al, our Director of Admissions, said, "You know it's years since I've seen such good-looking coeds?", and Eileen, who's an Assistant Dean, said, "Yeah, I've noticed that too. They're wearing skirts, they're wearing cute pant suits, they're wearing bright nail polish. Something's happening." And for almost three years now, the news has been coming in from all college campuses, that they're no longer looking like tramps any more, neither the men nor the women. Something is happening.

As you know for several years it was fashionable on college campuses for students to look like bums. The boys went around in ragged tennis shoes and dirty sweat shirts and the girls let their hair go untended and they wore ponchos over their fathers' worn-out shirts and went barefoot or in sandals. Pretty colors were "out" and smartness was out — even cleanliness was out.

And what was "in"? Synthetic poverty, that's what was in. Students with charge accounts, set up by their loving parents, at Marshall Fields or Saks Fifth Avenue, or Brooks Brothers, or Abercrombie & Fitch, in their scorn of "middle-class values", rejected such elegance, and wore blue jeans instead. And you remember the trying times that that offered to many students in the '60s. Unfortunately, new blue jeans looked new. Many young people were therefore put to the inconvenience of running their blue jeans repeatedly through the washing machine after splashing bleach and mud and so on on them. Ultimately they gave the blue jeans that desired beat-up look. At this point an alert clothing industry began to supply pre-faded, pre-soiled blue jeans at somewhat higher cost so that the wearer could look worn down by work and poverty, without ever having experienced either.

The late Eugene Burdick described in "The Subterraneans" how students at Berkeley in the 1960s would dig their hands into the dirt so that they could turn up in class with the proper amount of grime under their fingernails. Then there's that hippie girl, described by a San Diego columnist, getting out of a taxi at a freeway on-ramp, giving the driver a $10 bill saying "keep the change," and joining a group of her friends to hitchhike from there.

What an irony there is in this synthetic poverty game! In the 1930s poverty was really something to be feared. The national system of Social Security was just beginning. The poor were dependent on uncertain local charities.

Today, the poor have, comparatively, little to fear. There is welfare. There is Aid to Dependent Children. There are food stamps. Unemployment does not mean eviction and starvation, but unemployment checks.

Young people of the middle and upper-middle classes not only have not experienced poverty, they haven't even experienced the fear of poverty. When they have known

want, it was wanting a hi-fi stereo instead of the old-fash-
ioned monaural, or wanting an electric guitar instead of
the silly old kind Segovia plays.

Today, however, the synthetic poverty game seems to
be on the decline. As I said, the girls are looking pretty again.
They are washing their hair until it glows. Their styles are
not necessarily those of the fashion magazines, but many
are chic in their own way: some with ankle-length coats
over miniskirts, some with flared slacks with blouse and
leather vest, some with knit suits ornamented with "Afro"
or other hand-crafted jewelry.

And young men are wearing sports jackets, turtle necks,
colorful slacks. Some are even wearing neckties, attracted
by the colored-shirt and wide-necktie fad that has proved
so attractive to newscasters.

While all this is happening, intellectual changes are also
taking place. Students are crowding into career-oriented
programs: journalism, broadcasting, health sciences, business administration. What kind of job can you get with a
B.A. in English, they ask?

Thus, the old "middle-class values" so energetically rejected by elitist students in the 1960s are being reasserted.
There is little talk these days on revolution, of overthrowing
the Establishment. Posters of Che Guevara no longer grace
the walls of dormitory rooms. Leftovers from the revolution-
ary period of four years ago angrily denounce the present
student generation for "apathy."

But they do not seem apathetic to me. They are deeply
interested in problems of environment. They are concerned
with shortcomings in the fulfillment of the American dream.
But they do not believe that these problems can be solved by
blowing up the chemistry building. They believe in understanding problems in order to solve them. So they study.
Bless their hearts!

And, "middle-class values" are no longer scorned. Perhaps, students have realized that the hope of "the wretched of the earth" (as Franz Fanon called them) is that some day they might join the middle class. Perhaps, they have realized that the theoretical "classless society" of Marxist dreams is one in which there is no privileged aristocracy, no oppressed peasantry, but only one huge middle class.

Whatever the reasons, it has now become safe again to buy your college-age son a Countess Mara silk necktie and your college-age daughter a cashmere sweater from Sak's Fifth Avenue. Moderately happy days are here again.

You look back on those years and it's difficult to figure it out, but one way of throwing some light on this problem is to read the great Russian novelist, Turgenev and his book, *Fathers and Sons,* although written over 100 years ago, portraying the conflicting views of two generations. Then too the elite students, the college students, the university students, in Moscow, St. Petersburg, and so on, the younger generation of high-ranking officials, rich businessmen, generals in the Army, and other well-to-do parents, went radical. They became the roots of the Communist Revolution of 1917. They identified intensely with working classes and the peasants, and they dressed like peasants and the working classes and made heroes of them. They did much of what the American students did in the 1960s except it was much more dangerous then to do it. They started riots, they protested on behalf of the oppressed peasantry. And you know in Russia in those days the peasantry really *was* oppressed and it was something to complain about. But anyway, *if* they got arrested, they weren't immediately given amnesty, as American students demanded and got; they were often sent to Siberia or their careers were ruined. I mean they went to jail and some of them were shot. That's what Czarism was. Obviously, the identification of the children of the

well-to-do with the people at the bottom of the social ladder
— that's happened before. And what happened before in
Russia, also happened here, the people at the bottom of the
ladder, the actual peasants, distrusted the students, in the
same way that our working class in America distrusted the
student rebellion, too. Both the Russian peasants and our
working class had a sound intuition that these students,
sympathizing with their cause, weren't going to do them
any good in the long run—being considered a condescension.

This whole thing is a matter of a kind of elitism and
I'm afraid that we in the Humanities Departments are part-
ly responsible for inculcating it. First, the elitism comes from
being moderately well-to-do, or extremely well-to-do, as is
the case of The Weathermen and their underground population now. But it also comes from, well, an idea that Plato
more than anybody else crystallized for coming generations.
He said that philosophers should be kings. He dreamed of
a society of philosopher kings. So here you are, philosophy
major, literature major, sociology major, great, great in-
tellect, or at least you think you are, and you feel that those
who really understand should be kings. And they *despise*
the California Legislature, or the Tennessee Legislature —
as full of insurance men and hardware dealers and
auto supply people — crummy businessmen of all kinds.
They don't know anything. But we who are students of
philosophy and literature *do* understand deep moral issues,
more than those creeps in the legislatures. That's the general feeling but notice that the Student Movement which
was *said* to be political was, in a very important sense, anti-
political. They did not want to go through City Hall, they
did not want to go through the State Legislature, they did
not want to go through the Courts. They wanted to burn
down the R.O.T.C. Building, or blow up the Chemistry
Building, in order to stop the war in Vietnam or whatever

it was they felt they needed to do. They were totally anti-political.

It really shook me up the other day to read a magazine about Asian affairs. It said that the government of Singapore — I think the talk was about Singapore, it may have been Malaysia, but the same thing may also be true in South Korea — felt that in order to help their underdeveloped country achieve a higher development, they should make more and more universities and colleges open for people, increase their educational opportunities, and get the young, bright young people, into degree programs, and professional programs of all kinds. It was believed that if this happened the students seeing the rising prosperity of the entire nation would be very happy and go ahead and study their professional programs, grateful to the nation for what it did.

But, of course, the very opposite happened. In Singapore, and certainly it's true in South Korea, these students are rising up against the government. The President of Korea, Chang Hae Park, is having a rough time, Wang Ku Lee in Singapore is having also a tough time, and the student elitists are giving him the same kind of trouble. And when you think back again to the United States, where did the uproar start? It started in the prestige colleges with the highest admission standards, didn't it? At Columbia, Swarthmore, Harvard, Berkeley, Stanford. These are elite colleges, and there's where it started.

A common thread runs through those events. One of the real dangers of education is it makes some people feel that they're better than other people. Because you've got an M.A. or a B.A. or because you're a sophomore English major, somehow you begin to feel that you're a superior order of being to the man who pumps your gas at the service station, to the man who runs the department store downtown, or to the man who runs a lumber mill upstate. And we, who are intellectuals should be running the country. Philosopher-kings, that's what Plato said and boy, it's a dangerous idea.

Of course, Communism is very much the same kind of thing. It's always imposed from above by a bunch of intellectuals who feel they know better than the common people what's good for them. But the common people are illustrating right now in South Vietnam what they think of Communism, and many of them are illiterate peasants but they know enough to run away. And instead of welcoming their Communist liberators and the Liberation Movement, two million are fleeing the northern provinces of Vietnam for safety, even when they know there is no safety, they're fleeing anyway. By gosh, you know, the South Vietnam people inspire me very, very much as really, really freedom-loving people, as the Cambodians are. For three years the newspapers have been predicting the fall of Phenom Penh and even now, at this last deperate situation, it still hasn't fallen — or has it by this time? It hasn't, has it? And for the last two weeks, especially, reporters say, "It's gone, it's gone." They said it again this morning "It's gone." But why are they fighting so desperately? Well, they don't like their present government, perhaps, but they sure as hell don't like Communism any better, and they are fleeing.

I admire and respect the South Vietnamese for this fact. The common people have an awful lot of sense.

Anyway, let me go on. Henry David Thoreau, said more than a hundred years ago, that "Students should not play at life, or study it merely, while the community supports them at this expensive game, but earnestly live it from beginning to end. How could youths better learn to live than by at once trying the experiment of living." This is a very important point that Thoreau's making except he made it long ago when education wasn't nearly as expensive nor extensive as it is now.

Today, what's happening is that 75% of crimes in the street are committed by young people under 21, mostly men but sometimes women. Fourteen and fifteen year olds, boys and girls, pounce on elderly people in the streets and rob them. They're not content with robbing them, they sometimes beat them up and kill them too, after taking 7 bucks off them. And public schools and high schools are regularly vandalized by vicious youngsters, some as young as 10 or 11. The problem of our times, said Eric Hoffer in a speech in San Francisco not long ago, is the vast increase in the number of "teenagers." "We used to count as teenagers those between the ages of thirteen and nineteen. Now the teenage group includes those between the ages of ten and thirty. The post-Sputnik education explosion has been keeping students in their late twenties in college in a state of delayed manhood, while television is giving ten-year olds the life-style of juveniles. There are no children anymore. Our public schools are packed with mini-men and mini-women, hungering for the prerogatives and probably the responsibilities of adults."

One can add in support of Hoffer's observation that young people reach biological maturity much earlier than they did at the beginning of this century. Whether because of improved nutrition or other reasons, the fourteen-year old today, boy or girl, is biologically as mature as a sixteen-year old of 1910. This makes a great, great difference. At the same time that this is happening, of course, compulsory education goes on and on, long past fourteen. In 1910 a fourteen-year old was expected to leave school and go to work. A grade school education was considered enough for most people. Perhaps an eighth of the population went on to finish high school.

In the 1970s a fourteen-year-old, biologically equivalent

of a sixteen-year old in 1910 is faced with seven or eight more years of schooling, if college-bound (and in California more than 50% are), before being launched into the adult world — and longer than that if he wants to go into the professions.

However, not all the young are studiously inclined, at least not in the direction of academic accomplishments. Many will not be interested or ready for academic studies until they're in their twenties or thirties, if at all. In the meantime they're interested in becoming racing drivers, ball players, forest-rangers, body-and-fender men, mechanics, horsemen and horsewomen, actors and actresses and models. They have all sorts of aspirations for which academic training is only marginally necessary. Yet we keep them in school whether they like it or not.

Meanwhile, says Hoffer, "The mini-men, bored by meaningless book-learning are hungry for action, hungry to acquire all sorts of skills." For such young people, schools are prisons. They are sick of preparing for life. They want to live.

Hoffer believes that schooling should be limited to four hours a day: "It should consist of reading and writing, elementary mathematics, a familiarization with the geography of the planet, and a bird's-eye view of history. There is evidence that a student in his twenties, when he's eager to learn, can master in less than a year, all the book-learning that teachers try to force into unwilling minds in grammar and high schools." Hoffer may be right on that.

But after four hours, he says, students should spend the rest of the day at useful tasks. They would build houses and roads. They would clear the forest. They would learn gardening and landscaping. They would learn to operate and take care of machinery. (Incidentally have you noticed how thrilled teenage boys are whenever they are taught to use

power tools and given responsibility for them? Power tools
are the great fascination of young men now-a-days.) Hoffer
suggests that retired carpenters, masons, plumbers, electri-
cians and so on, be hired, to teach the young their crafts.
Students should build, he says, housing projects, housing
for the poor. Indeed they should plan and build whole
neighborhoods. Then, says Hoffer, "When they graduate
from school, they should be equipped not only to earn a
living, but to run the world. They should receive a graduation diploma and a union card at the same time."

Professor Neil Postman of New York University has
another idea about how to take up this lag, this problem of
adolescence. Professor Postman is eloquent on the frustrations of the young. He wrote a book called, *Education as a
Subversive Activity,* and in a fantasy Postman imagines what
it would be like if New York school children from the seventh
through the twelfth grade were to be given real responsibilities for the health and livability of New York City. This is
what he says, "So the curriculum of the public schools of
New York City became known as Operational Survival . . .
On Monday morning of each week, four hundred thousand
children had to help clean up their own neighborhoods. They
swept the streets, they canned the garbage, removed the litter
from the empty lots . . . Wednesday mornings were reserved
for beautifying the city. They planted trees and flowers, they
repainted the subway stations, and so on . . . Each day five
thousand students had to help direct traffic on city streets
so that policemen could be free to fight crime. And each day
five thousand students were asked to help deliver the mail . . .
Several thousand students were also used to establish and
maintain day-care centers . . . Each student was also assigned
to meet with two elementary school students on Tuesday
and Thursday afternoon to teach them to read, write and
do arithmetic . . . "

In Postman's fantasy, he says, "Most of the students found that while they did not *receive* an education, they were able to *create* quite adequately. They lived, each day, their social studies, their hygiene, their geography, their communication, their biology, their political science and many other things that decent and proper people know about, including the belief that everyone must share equally in creating a livable New York City."

It's understandable that Eric Hoffer, a loyal Union man and longshoreman, should hope that trade unions would ultimately help solve the problems of our adolescents and that they would undertake, in cooperation with the schools, major responsibilities for the future of young people. But the aspirations he has for the young, no less than the aspirations of Professor Neil Postman, are impossible of achievement in today's world. Well, why? Well, if you want to pick up the garbage, and can it, and get it out of the streets and so on, what do you run into? You run into the obstacles of The Garbagemen's Union first of all; they've got a monopoly on moving the garbage; then you run into the Postal Union on moving and delivering the mail; and you run into the Policemen's Union on directing traffic; and so on and so on, with one obstacle after another, including the tremendous obstacles the unions themselves generally place in the way of jobs for growing boys and girls. The frustrations of the young are enormous. These union regulations, combined with minimum wage laws, child labor laws, school attendance laws, employers' liability insurance practices, and community pressures keep the young out of the labor market, and therefore in a state of frustration, and so they've got to go to school, whether they like it or not. I think this is disastrous.

Young people need challenges. For many young people the academic life *is* challenging indeed and they love it, but the whole problem of being a young person, in his teens, is that his whole being cries out for challenges. For, let's say a young man to face starvation, to face the possibility of death at enemy hands, to face the risks of failure in school or business and then to triumph over these dangers, these are the very stuff of human growth, human development.

Nevertheless, the vast majority of young people are excluded from the adult world and denied the chance to exercise their powers, physical or intellectual. So is it any wonder there's a youth problem? For many young people high school is no challenge. In many communities if you don't learn enough to get in to the next grade, they pass you anyway. If there's no such thing as failure, what kind of achievement is it to have passed? And our extremely permissive educational system, by destroying failure, — I learned that the "F" is almost unheard of in the university grading system now-a-days — if there's no such thing as "failure", what is the meaning of "success", what's the meaning of "passing"?

For many the curriculum in high school is so slow and repetitive that it's a bore. For others, it's simply meaningless. David Reisman says "What young men and women need, as they grow up, is to be extended to the limit of their powers." But what is there in a boy's life, in our affluent society, to extend him to the limit of his powers? If he gets on the high school football team, then he will be extended to the limit of his powers, but that's a small minority in any high school. Therefore, if socially acceptable forms of real life activity are denied the young through protracted schooling, they are driven by inner necessity to illegal activities, whether car theft, assault and robbery, experiments with drugs, or blowing up the R.O.T.C. Building. You see, just as babies need love, young people growing into maturity need challenges.

Considering the obstacles to maturity that stand in the way of young people today, Eric Hoffer says, "What this country needs and can have is child labor." And I would say to Mr. Hoffer, I agree with you. Tell it to the longshoremen's union that hasn't let in a new member, I understand, for thirty years in San Francisco. Then have the longshoremen talk to all the other unions. The union members' own children are getting into trouble out of this kind of frustration.

What Neil Postman and Eric Hoffer say about the problems of education is so true. Must education, whether in high school or college, be so exclusively by the book? All too often education appears to be, as the semantists say, words, and words about words, and words about words about words. There's no doubt that books illuminate life. But if students are not permitted to experience life, what is there for the books to illuminate? Some of you may have had the experience of teaching, let us say, the same work of literature, let's say *King Lear* to a high school class and to an adult education class. The emotions in *King Lear* are too complex for a high school class to understand, they're bored stiff. But when people are over thirty, or over forty, they can understand *King Lear*. And then this lesson plan that didn't work at all in high school, suddenly works in adult education, because they're mature enough to understand.

For reasons such as those, experimental high schools and colleges throughout the country are taking their students out into the community, actively involving them in life outside the classroom. I hope something of this kind is going on here. They're given chores to do in city offices, jobs in factories, department stores, social agencies and hospitals, responsibilities for tutoring elementary school children — then they meet to discuss their experiences and to get reading assignments. Thereby, the reading and the study tie in with real life experiences. I think that's a good thing. I would hope that as time goes on, education will become more and

more involved with the total community. There should be
thousands of part-time students active in the life of the city.
There should be cooperation between the colleges and the
social agencies and hospitals and industry. Institutions of
higher education in great urban centers should become less
and less ivory towers and more and more a force in the world.
Because our mature young men and women from fifteen to
nineteen or twenty are ready to take an active, responsible
part in life — and we don't let them, we have a real Achilles
heel of our civilization.

More than a hundred years ago, American schools took
a great step forward toward the democratizing of higher education when the Morrill Act of 1862 authorized land-grant
colleges in every state of the Union. This destroyed the
monopoly of the private schools like Harvard and Princeton
and gave Minnesota and Nebraska, and all sorts of far out
places a state university. Over the past century these institutions proliferated and grew into the great agricultural and
mechanical colleges and the state universities of today. They
were the principal agencies through which an entirely new
educated class was created in the United States. You see,
as our industry grew, as our prosperity grew, as our opportunities grew, there had to be an educated class, through
Schools of Mining, Schools of Agriculture, Schools of Technology, and so on. And then there had to be the professors
of all the Liberal Arts too to take care of all the cultural
needs of the nation. And so the development over the last
hundred years of the entire system of higher education in
the United States, including Memphis State University, the
University of California, of Wisconsin, of Minnesota, of
Purdue, and all other great institutions — that's something
we should all be very proud of. No other nation in the world
has anything to approach this kind of educational system,
except as the result of the American Occupation of Japan,

we taught the Japanese that they ought to have distinguished institutions all over their country, not only in Tokyo and Kyoto and so now there are great universities all through Japan. That's a very good thing.

Thus, what's happening today is the further democratization of higher education. The next great instrument with which America continues to expand educational opportunities for all the people is the two-year or community college. In 1960, that's a very short time ago, there were 521 community colleges in the United States. In 1970, the number had grown to 827. Today there are probably a thousand, perhaps over a thousand, virtually all of them growing at a furious rate. Some of these are fantastically large institutions, like the junior college system of Miami, Florida, or of Jacksonville, Florida; and the junior college system constitutes about ninety institutions in California alone. Now how many do you have in this state? You have quite a large number developing, have you not? Anyway, the junior college movement is the exciting, big thing that's happening. The enrollment figures are impressive too: In 1960, 451,000 students were going to community colleges. In 1965, five years later, 841,000; in 1970 there were 1,630,000; in 1972 there were 1,792,000 students. The thing continues to proliferate. That is, the population of junior colleges, multiplied by a factor of 4, in the period of some twelve years.

Here are a few more facts: From 1960 to '72 students in American colleges and universities increased from 3.6 million to 8.3 million. In 1940, a majority of young Americans, 55%, failed to finish high school; by 1972 that percentage had dropped to 25%. These figures are quite meaningful. Ben Wattenberg in *The Real America* writes: "Expenditures for education, mostly coming from self-imposed taxes levied by local and state governments closest to the people, have soared from 9 billion dollars in 1950 to

25 billion in 1960, to 86 billion in 1972 . . . " (We're just blowing our money right and left on higher education, on education in general.) "The magnitude of the expansion of the college system in America in the last decade is hard to overestimate. In terms of money spent, it far dwarfs the Manhattan Project, putting a man on the Moon, and from the years 1965 to 1972, was somewhat larger than the Vietnam War."

What is the result of all this experience, of all this expenditure? More people than ever from poor families are going to college. Wattenberg gives one figure that really startled me: "Today, about 60% of college students are from families where the head of the household had not completed a single year of college. (See, that means that a generation of high school graduates are going to have children who are college graduates.) And today, 21% of young people from homes with family incomes from 3,000 to 5,000 dollars are enrolled in college, (Isn't that fantastic?) — a larger rate than the TOTAL figure for either France or Germany or England or Italy!"

Community colleges, which have contributed much to this education explosion, have attracted not only the young of every income level, but the mature — and that is the very interesting thing. They have enrolled a remarkable mix of people of all ages: teenagers, veterans, retired military, adults seeking a change of job. Mature women have enrolled in large numbers — young mothers as well as older women, driven sometimes by ambition, sometimes by intellectual curiosity, or even the simple desire to get out of the house as the children grow older.

There was an advertisement in *McCalls* not long ago. That's one of the learned journals I look into occasionally. There was an advertisement in *McCalls* that said: "I was a graying, overweight mother of three, and now I'm a college freshman." You see, you put Clairol on her head, and she felt young, and she enrolled in college as a freshman. She started life all over again. But as a person interested in education, especially in community college. That ad fascinated me—an advertisement which legitimizes all sorts of behavior. That's one of the functions of advertising, to legitimize various kinds of behavior. And it was saying to a graying mother, tied up in her housework ,and having given up intellectual hopes for herself: "Look, you put on some Clairol, freshen yourself up, reduce, go back to college. Start a whole new career, a whole new life." That's a fantastic thing that our business system is doing. Incredible!

While all this was happening in the last twelve years, what was the prevailing intellectual fashion? It always amazes me how tremendously distant the actual motivations of the people are from the fashions that go in the intellectual world— *The New York Review of Books,* and other such highbrow magazines. Colleges and universities were denounced by radical, chic ideologists as unresponsive to social needs, irrelevant, resistant to social change, and structured through "institutional racism" to exclude minorities and the poor. Indeed, the university system, including the community colleges, have been tremendously responsive to social needs as you can tell by their simple growth since 1960. They have not at all been resistant to social change. They have produced a fantastic amount of social change on their own. And they are not structured through "institutional racism" to exclude minorities and the poor. They welcomed the minorities and have given them great new opportunities and they have made the poor less poor by opening new doors of opportunity to them.

Wattenberg's statistics confirm my own teaching experience over the past thirty-five years in public institutions. What we've experienced in the past twelve years especially is another great breakthrough in popular education in which the promises of American democracy are being realized as never before. And I think we have reason, as Americans, to congratulate ourselves on that record.